VORTIGERN

An Investigation from the Sources

Janice Van Cleve

Additional Books by the author:

Incidents of Travel in Mesoamerica (2017)

The Jumanji Passport vol. 2 (2017)

The Jumanji Passport vol. 1 (2016)

Tikal: Turning Point (2018)

The Kings Of Copan In Their Own Words (2015)

Eighteen Rabbit – The Intimate Life And Tragic Death Of A Maya God-King. (2006)

The Founder – The Life Of Yax Kuk Mo, Mover And Shaker In The Maya World (2010)

Maya Investigations Vol. 1 (2014)

Dandelion – A Children's Book For Grownups, Too! (2013)

America: Course Correction (2011)

Sound And Summits (2014)

Brain Farts (2020)

Table of Contents

Preface

The scant and conflicting contemporary narratives of 5th
Century Britain often leave as much space for speculation
as they do for confirmed fact. Many historians and
novelists have written about Arthur and some touch upon
the period immediately before him, but only a few serious
researchers have dug deeper. The most instructive may be
found on a website dedicated to the period called Vortigern
Studies at www.vortigernstudies.org.

This present investigation focuses on original sources in
combination with later research to examine significant
events in the life of Vortigern. The sources are very few.
They sometimes conflict, sometimes include extraneous
material – even fables – and in some cases contain outright
fabrications. The evaluation of Vortigern's reign follows in
the last chapter.

Britain in the 4th Century was a prosperous and mostly
peaceful province of the Roman empire. It even supplied
grain to the legions on the Rhine frontier. However, as one
Roman general after another drained troops from the island
to fight for the imperial throne in Rome, the island's
defenses were weakened. Picts from the north and Scotti
from Ireland began to raid. The British landowners called
on Rome for help and one detachment did come back and
routed the raiders in 418, but when they left no further help
was offered. Rome had troubles of its own. The Eternal
City had been sacked by the Visigoths in 410. Attila the
Hun with his Germanic allies was invading western Europe
and he was only stopped in 451. Britain was on its own.

Little is known for sure about the history of Britain from 418 to the reign of Alfred the Great, king of Wessex (871-886) and later king of all the Anglo Saxons (886-899). What chronicles and records did exist were destroyed or lost in the raids and battles of the period. Several monks and clerics did try to pull together a history from scattered sources they could gather.

The author is deeply indebted to Robert Vermaat and the website www.vortigernstudies.org which he edits. Vermaat has created a rich resource for the study of early British history including an exhaustive bibliography, key articles, and his own research. The author has in her library most of the primary and secondary sources cited herein and the interpretations she presents are entirely her own.

- Janice Van Cleve 2020

Primary Sources

Prosper of Aquitaine, a prolific writer of ecclesiastical tracts, wrote a contemporary chronicle covering events from 433 to 455, including the visit of Germanus to Britain.

Gallic Chronicle CCCCLII, by a contemporary of Prosper, focused on the barbarian invasions of the crumbling Roman empire up to 452, including Saxon invasions of Britain.

Gallic Chronicle DXI, by a writer in southern Gaul, continued Chronicle CCCCLII up to 511.

Constantius of Lyon, a monk who wrote the <u>Life of St. Germanus</u> sometime between 460 and 480, related the visit of bishop Germanus to Britain in 429 to combat Pelagianism.   There is no evidence that Constantius visited Britain in person but he was a friend of Bishop Lupus of Troyes who accompanied Germanus on his visit to Britain.

Gildas, a British monk, composed <u>De Exidio Britanniae</u> sometime between 510-530 in Wales or Cornwall. It is a sermon excoriating the British kings and clergy and not a history. He mentions Vortigern and the Battle of Badon.

Bede, composed <u>History of the English Church and People</u> in 731 in Saxon Northrumbia. He copied from Gildas and Constantius when he wrote about Vortigern and the coming of the Saxons.

Nennius wrote his <u>History of the Britons</u> in 945 in south Wales and his is the most detailed account of Vortigern, gleaned from what appears to have been a collection of sources, some of which are fables, but nevertheless a valuable and detailed resource.

The Pillar of Eliseg, erected in Powys during the time of Nennius, records a lineage of rulers back to Vortigern.

Anglo-Saxon Chronicle, compiled under the auspices of Alfred the Great in the latter part of the 9th Century, briefly covers history from the beginning of the Current Era but becomes more detailed after 400.

Annales Cambriae, compiled in the 10th Century, is mainly a collection of Welsh history. Entries are brief and cryptic starting with 447CE.

William of Malmesbury, a monk of Malmesbury Abbey in Wiltshire, finished his <u>History of the English Kings</u> in 1125 and is considered one of England's best historians. As librarian for the abbey, William had direct access to hundreds of sources.

Geoffrey of Monmouth, a Welsh cleric and magister at Oxford completed his <u>History of the Kings of Britain</u> in 1136. He is primarily responsible for his highly romanticized presentation of Arthur, who was becoming legendary by the 12th Century.

Vortigern's Britain 380 - 447

Vortigern's origins

Nennius liked genealogies and listed a long one for Vortigern's family. They were apparently among the elite of the Cornovii tribe which had been allies of the Romans. He located them around the area of Gwent in southeast Wales and notes that four of the brothers built the city of Gloucester on the Severn River, naming it Cair Gloui, after their predecessor Gloui. The Cornovii homeland generally extended over the whole Severn river valley and its tributaries which became the area of medieval Powys. Its capital was the Roman city of Virconium Cornoviorum (modern Wroxter), which at its height, was the 4th largest Roman city in Britain. Modern archeology has shown evidence of a major rebuilding at Virconium beginning about 420, when Vortigern was advancing his power.

The Pillar of Eliseg is a stone monument in north Wales with an inscription that ends with: "Britu, son of Vortigern whom Germanus blessed and whom Severa bore to him, the daughter of Maximus the king, who killed the king of the Romans". Maximus was a Roman general who led an army from Britain in 383 to claim the imperial throne. He defeated and killed emperor Gratian. The eastern Roman emperor objected to this and had Maximus executed five years later. The Pillar of Eliseg implies that he left a daughter back in Britain when he went off to war and she married Vortigern and bore his son, Britu. Thus by this marriage Vortigern could claim some legitimacy to rule.

At the end of his book (chapter 66) Nennius identifies the beginning of Vortigern's reign the same year that Roman Emperor Valentinian III assumed the throne in Rome – 425 CE. Valentinian III was only 6 years old when he came to the throne of the Western Roman Empire in 425 and was under the regency of his powerful mother, Galla Placidia, until his 18th birthday in 436. He ruled alone until his assassination in 455.

Nennius writes "Also from Stilicho to Valentinian, son of Placidia, and the reign of Vortigern, are twenty eight years." Stilicho was executed in 408. Adding 28 years brings us to 436, about the time that Valentinian came of age. Nennius does not state that Vortigern's rule began in 436 but that he was in power in 436. If the 28 years is counted from Stilicho's consulship in 400, we arrive at 428, still within Vortigern's reign. In chapter 31 he states that Britain was "in alarm forty years" after the death of Maximus in 388. In the next sentence, he writes "Vortigern then reigned in Britain." Forty years after 388 is 428, again pointing to Vortigern already in power.

Vortigern's family

When Vortigern was born is not documented. He married
Severa, who must at least have been born before 383 when
her father Maximus left her in Britain and went off to
Rome. Therefore Vortigern must have been born not too
many years before or after 383. In chapter 47 Nennius
identifies three sons of Vortigern – Vortimer, Categirn, and
Pascent – presumably by Severa. Vortimer succeeded his
father and was probably killed in a battle. Categirn was
killed at the battle of Aylesford. Pascent survived until
Ambrosius the Younger became ruler. As a peace gesture
between his family and the Vortigern clan, Ambrosius
granted Pascent the counties of Builth and Guorthegirnaim
in Powys (now in south central Wales) and he is named in
the genealogy listed on the Pillar of Eliseg.

Vortigern also had a daughter, Scotnoe, whowas married
off to the son of the Irish king. Nennius claims another
unnamed daughter who supposedly bore him a son,
Faustus, by incest. Neither Gildas, nor Bede, nor Geoffrey
mention this incest. William repeats Nennius' allegation.
This is probably a fable to vilify Vortigern and to glorify
bishop Germanus who supposedly took the boy and raised
him back in his see at Auxerre. Nennius claims Faustus
later founded a monastery on the banks of the river Renis in
southern France. Vermaat notes that Bishop Faustus of
Riez may be the same Faustus, son of Vortigern, who may
have been a conduit for news of British events to the Gallic
Chroniclers. As an aside, Gildas calls Vortigern *infaustus*

which means unfortunate; *"faustus"* in Latin means fortunate.

Vermaat lists five sons for Vortigern – Vortimer, Pascent, Categirn, Faustus, Britu, and a daughter, Scotnoe. He does not list a second daughter and he dismisses the incest story as a fabrication. Nennius does not mention Britu but the Pillar of Eliseg does. Phillips and Keatman propose that Vortimer is a title held by Britu and that he became a second Vortigern after his father was deposed. David Ford, in the Vortigern Studies, asserts that Britu could not have been Vortimer but rather a younger brother. However, the <u>Anglo-Saxon Chronicle</u> records the Battle of Aylesford in 455 in which Hengist and Horsa battled somebody named Vortigern. If Vortigern was born around 380, he certainly would not still be around in 455 fighting battles at 75 years of age. It is more likely that a second Vortigern fought the battle and Britu (now the new Vortigern) is the most likely candidate.

Vortigern also married Renwein, daughter of the Saxon chief, Hengist, sometime between 431 and 436. Neither Gildas nor Bede mention her but Nennius does and Geoffrey elaborates. According to Geoffrey, after she poisoned Britu, she encouraged Vortigern to bring his nobles to her father's banquet where they were killed. Vermaat says it is more likely that Britu was killed in battle sometime in the late 450's and Renwein returned to her father after the banquet which probably occurred in the mid-440's.

Vortigern as Overlord

"Vortigern" is not a personal name yet neither is it a formal title. Vermaat calls it a claim to overlordship. Morris calls it a nickname, something like "The Man". Vortigern's son and successor, Britu, was also called "Vortigern" when he took over from his father. Before then, Britu was called "Vortimer" by the monks writing about him. If "Vortigern" is a claim to overlordship, "Vortimer" may be a claim to heir apparent. We do not know Vortigern's personal name although Vermaat theorizes that he may have had a Roman name, Vitalinus, but offers that only as an opinion. Ashley offers a suggestion that Vortigern's name may have been Cunorix.

Although the monks writing this early history call Vortigern a king, the institution of kingship was not fully formed at this early date. Vortigern was the overlord, but he held that position as a first among equals. Gildas in chapter 23 writes that "All the counselors, together with that proud tyrant Gurthrigen (Vortigern), the British king, invited the Saxons". Bede writes in chapter 14 "all agreed with the advice of their king, Vortigern, to call on the assistance of the Saxon people". We do not know the nature and function of this council, but it probably included the major landowners, aristocrats, and petty chieftains. A diminished but still lingering local Roman officialdom and governing style still existed in Britain for awhile after the Roman legions left.

Vortigern was only grudgingly accepted by the upper class
landowners and officials in Britain. Morris claims that not
only did they regard him as an uncouth barbarian, a social
climber, and an upstart, they especially despised the way he
openly played to the urban poor and to the farm workers.
They recoiled at his preference for Celtic language and
manners instead of Roman ones. He may also have been a
Pagan or a Pelagian which would have put him at odds with
the Roman bishops. Vortigern's nativism ran counter to the
aristocracy's more cosmopolitan imperial notions and it
undercut the aristocrats' social standing in a country where
they were fast becoming foreigners. Nennius says of
Vortigern: "In his time, the natives had cause of dread, not
only from the inroads of the Scots (Irish) and Picts, but also
from the Romans, and their apprehensions of Ambrosius."

Ambrosius the Elder was leader of the aristocratic
opposition. He appears to have been a Roman, rather than
a Romano-Briton, and he held an official position based on
London. Gildas writes that he "wore the purple" signifying
consular rank. He was an important member of the council
and a potential threat to Vortigern's rule. His son,
Ambrosius the Younger, assumed leadership of the Britons
in 460.

Thus Vortigern was at odds with the church and the
aristocrats and faced foreign invasions as well. That he
survived around twenty years in power in spite of these
handicaps is some testament to his skill or luck.

Bishop Germanus

Bishop Germanus (378-450) enters the story of Vortigern in 429. He was a lawyer, soldier, and Roman official married to Eustachia, a woman connected in imperial circles. He was consecrated bishop of Auxerre in 418 (folklore says he was tricked or shoved into the priesthood) and proceeded to employ his considerable talents to church administration. Constantius makes no mention of children and apparently he remained married. In those times, church and state were so entwined that men of talent were often recruited to serve in both capacities simultaneously, married or not.

In 429 Germanus was sent to Britain to confront Pelagianism, which denied the doctrine of original sin. While there he instituted the cult of St. Alban. Constantius reports that some Britons, faced with a raid by Saxons and Picts in north Wales, asked Germanus to use his military experience to lead an army against the enemy. The legend claims he did and won the victory by shouting Alleluia! which frightened the enemy and won the battle. However Constantius may have confused Germanus with Guithelinus, bishop of London, who Geoffrey states sought troops from Brittany to defeat the Picts sometime before Vortigern came to power. Bede repeats the Constantius' battle story in chapter 20 and then reports that Germanus returned to Auxerre in 429. Constantius, on the other hand, writes in chapter 16 that Germanus had a fall and injured his foot. "the bishop was detained by his injury in one place for a considerable period". It is likely that Germanus spent more than one year in Britain.

Nennius claims that Germanus was "unanimously chosen commander against the Saxons" after the second banquet with Hengist (see below) and only then won the Alleluia battle. So Nennius places the Alleluia battle during the second visit by Germanus in 447 while Bede places the Alleluia battle during his first visit in 429. Nennius writes that Germanus destroyed Benlii, a local chief based at Moel Fenli in north Powys, during his first visit. Germanus reportedly brought down fire from heaven and burned Benlii in his city. Then Germanus appointed Catel, one of the chief's servants, to be the new king of Powys, according to Nennius.

Bede also takes Constantius at face value in relating a second visit by Germanus to Britain and dates it between 435 and 444. Prosper of Aquitaine's chronicle from 433 to 444 does not mention a second visit, and Gildas does not mention the bishop at all – even though he does mention St. Alban. The <u>Anglo-Saxon Chronicle</u> does not mention Germanus or any visits by the bishop.

The <u>Life of St. Germanus</u> as told by Constantius is a hagiography, not a solid history. Later monks picked up on his miracles and attributed events to him to promote the church agenda. Hence the Alleluia battle and the similar destructions of both Benlii and Vortigern in their strongholds by heavenly fire are fiction. There is no direct evidence that Germanus met or had any interaction with Vortigern. Britu, after he took over from his father, may have reconciled with the church to secure its support in his fight against the Saxons. If Germanus was involved in this reconciliation, it could only have happened during the

second visit by the bishop. The Pillar of Eliseg hints at
this.

Pillar of Eliseg

The Pillar of Eliseg is a stone monument in northeast Wales erected by Concenn, king of Powys, in the early 9th Century in honor of his great grandfather Eliseg. The cross that used to crown its top was broken off in the English Civil War. The inscription has long since been eroded but enough was clear in 1662 for Robert Vaughan make a copy.   An antiquarian, Edward Lhuyd, transcribed Vaughan's copy in 1696.

The generally accepted translation of the Latin reads:

"Concenn son of Cattell, Cattell son of Brochmail, Brochmail son of Eliseg, Eliseg son of Guoillauc. And that Concenn, great-grandson of Eliseg, erected this stone for his great-grandfather Eliseg. The same Eliseg, who joined together the inheritance of Powys . . . throughout nine (years?) out of the power of the Angles with his sword and with fire. Whosoever shall read this hand-inscribed stone, let him give a blessing on the soul of Eliseg. This is that Concenn who captured with his hand eleven hundred acres which used to belong to his kingdom of Powys . . .and which . . . .the mountain . . .

[the pillar is broken here and one or more lines may have been lost]
. . .the monarchy . . . Maximus of Britain . . . nn Pascent . . Maun Annan . . . Britu son of Vortigern, whom Germanus blessed, and whom Severa bore him, daughter of Maximus the king, who killed the king of the Romans."

The pillar gives no date for Germanus blessing Britu but in a footnote to chapter 44 in Nennius, the translator, J. A. Giles, observes that some manuscript copies of chapter 44 include a gloss in the margin that tells of a synod at Guartherniaun in Wales. At the synod, Britu reportedly fell at the feet of Germanus and begged pardon for his father's wickedness and gave the church a portion of land. Left unsaid is the blessing Germanus gave Britu for the apology and the gift. Vermaat notes that the gloss is a late addition to the text about 1200 or 370 years after Nennius wrote his history. This sounds suspiciously that the gloss is a retrofit by some clergy to justify a land claim and not an accurate record of real events. It is also suspicious that the Abbey of Valle Crucis where the pillar stands was also founded that same year, in 1200.

The gloss, however, does not discount the pillar which was erected almost 400 years earlier. If Germanus was in Britain in 429 – when Vortigern was at the fullness of his control – it is unlikely that he would have allowed his son to be blessed or that Britu would have had the freedom of action to receive a blessing. It is more likely that the blessing happened after Vortigern was deposed, which would mean that Germanus must have returned to Britain as Bede reports in chapter 21. Germanus arrived in Milan in 448 and he died in Ravenna in 450. Concenn died while on pilgrimage to Rome in 854. His father Cadell died in 808.

Arrival of the Saxons

The date of the first arrival of the Saxons in Britain
depends on whom you ask. To begin with, some writers
date by consular year which begins when the Roman
consuls took office on January 1. However, the church new
year began on March 15. Also dating from the incarnation
of Christ (anywhere between 4 BCE and 4 CE) or the
passion of Christ (sometime between 28 and 33 CE) also
affected the dates. This explains some variation in dates in
the sources.

Bede (chapter 15, book 1) writes "In the year of our Lord
449, Martian became Emperor with Valentinian and 46th
successor to Augustus, ruling for seven years. In his time
the Angles or Saxons came to Britain at the invitation of
King Vortigern in three long ships." Marcianus did indeed
become emperor of the Eastern Roman Empire in 450 and
did rule for seven years. Valentinian had been ruling on his
own since 436 and he was assassinated in 455. Therefore
the window Bede allows for the Saxons to arrive while both
emperors were ruling is the 5 years between 450 and 455.

In chapter 14 of book 2, Bede writes "King Edwin . . . in
the eleventh year of his reign, which was the year 627, and
about one hundred and eighty years after the first arrival of
the English in Britain." This casts back to the date of 447.
Bede not only mentions that they came in three long ships,
but he also identifies their leaders as Hengist and Horsa.

The <u>Anglo-Saxon Chronicle</u> copies Bede. The Chronicle lists the arrival of the Saxons in three long ships and their welcome by Vortigern in 449.

Gildas writes that the Battle of Badon in which the Britons crushed the Saxons "was 44 years and one month after the landing of the Saxons, and also the time of my own nativity." The <u>Annales Cambriae</u> lists the Battle of Badon at 516 which, if Gildas is to be believed, would put the arrival of the Saxons at 472, a date obviously far too late. Bede (chapter 16 book 1) copies Gildas that the battle of Badon took place 44 years after the arrival of the invaders, but he claims the battle occurred in 493, which takes the arrival of the Saxons back to his date in 449. Ashley convincingly calculates Gildas' birth in the early 490's.

However the Gallic Chronicles record the Saxons far earlier. Chronicle 452, entry 408/410: "The Britains were devastated by an incursion of the Saxons". Also entry 441: "The Britains, which to this time had suffered from various disasters and misfortunes, are reduced to the power of the Saxons." Chronicle 511, entry 440: "The Britians, lost to the Romans, yield to the power of the Saxons." Vermaat concludes that these contemporaneous accounts outweigh Bede's faulty calculations

Gildas himself writes in chapter 23 "They first landed on the eastern side of the island, by the invitation of the unfortunate king (Vortigern) . . .Their mother-land, finding her first brood thus successful, sends forth a larger company of her wolfish offspring, which sailing over, join themselves to their bastard-born comrades." Besides illustrating the vitriolic tone of Gildas' work, this passage indicates repeated landings of Saxons in Britain. The <u>Anglo-Saxon Chronicle</u> does not mention the Battle of

Badon because the chronicle is a Saxon account which does not record their defeats.

Nennius is confusing. In chapter 31 he writes "In the meantime, three vessels, exiled from Germany, arrived in Britain. They were commanded by Horsa and Hengist, brothers, and sons of Wihtgils . . . .Vortigern received them as friends, and delivered up to them the island which is in their language called Thanet, and, by the Britons, Ruym. Gratianus Aequantius at that time reigned in Rome. The Saxons were received by Vortigern, four hundred and forty seven years after the passion of Christ, and, according to the tradition of our ancestors, from the period of their first arrival in Britain, to the first year of the reign of king Edmund, five hundred and forty-two years."

Nennius does not add the traditional year of the passion (c. 33CE) to 447. Rather he is saying in the year 447, after Easter. That date coincides with Bede. However King Edmund I's reign began in 940. Minus 542 years gets to 398 which is too early (however, the Edmund reference does not appear in all copies of Nennius' work and can be ignored). Veprauskas disputes Giles' translation and argues that the original Latin text reads 347, not 447, and further that possible corruption of the Roman numerals yields 397. Add 32 to that and we come to 429 – four years after beginning of Vortigern's rule. His argument may or may not be valid but without Nennius' original, it cannot be determined.

The dates in Nennius' chapter 31 make no sense with chapter 66 in which he writes "Vortigern reigned in Britain when Theodosius and Valentinian were consuls and in the fourth year of his reign the Saxons came to Britain in the consulship of Felix and Taurus, in the four hundredth year from the incarnation of our Lord Jesus Christ." Roman records show Felix and Taurus were consuls together for the year 428. That fits with Nennius's earlier date of the beginning of Vortigern's reign in 425 and it fits with the reigns of Theodosius II (408-450) and Valentinian III (425-455).

As for Gratianus Aequantius, there is no emperor in Rome in the 5th century named Gratianus. There was a Gratian but he was overthrown by Maximus in 383. Nor is there a consul in Rome by that name. Geoffrey writes that a freedman named Gratianus, led a Roman relief force to Britain but well before the death of Maximus. Bede briefly mentions a Gratianus Municeps (chapter 11, book 1) who set himself up as Dictator (of Municipium, a Roman city of Verulamium located SW of St. Albans) in 407. He was soon killed, replaced by Constantine III, who crossed over into Gaul, set himself up as emperor at Arles and was also killed. Gratianus Municep was long dead before Horsa and Hengist arrived. Nennius' offhanded mention of him in chapter 31 probably reflects his scattered attempt to record anything he could find without discernment.

Veprauskas takes into account that Bede is writing from a Saxon perspective while Nennius is writing from a Welsh perspective. Bede may equate the first arrival of the Saxons to the time they invaded in large numbers to settle while Nennius may equate the first arrival to the time they landed as a smaller group of mercenaries and raiders. Whatever the case, Nennius is drawing from several sources and instead of making a decision, includes them both while Bede conflates the story of Hengist and Horsa with his story of the larger arrival later. The weight of evidence favors Nennius's final verdict: Vortigern becomes an overlord in 425 and four years later welcomes three boatloads of Saxons led by Horsa and Hengist.

Vortigern's Strategy

While Gildas generously calls Vortigern unfortunate, the other monks writing about him are less charitable. However, judging by the problems he faced and the actions he took, he made some adroit strategic moves. Invasions claimed Vortigern's first attention. His power base in Powys was vulnerable from north Wales and the Irish Sea. Irish, Pict, and Saxon raiders moved into that region as soon as the Romans left and began to build their strength – a strength that, if it came together in alliance, could overthrow Vortigern's budding kingdom.

John Morris in his exhaustive book <u>The Age of Arthur</u> gives credit to the Alleluia battle and the Benlii affair as part of Vortigern's developing strategy. He asserts that Germanus conducted both campaigns with the approval of Vortigern in trade for the latter's support for Patrick, Germanus' disciple, to preach in Ireland. According to Morris, relations between Vortigern and bishop Germanus were at least cooperative if not cordial. He asserts that the British episcopate was jealous of this outsider from Gaul and convinced Vortigern to raid Ireland as well. So Vortigern encouraged the slave raids of Coroticus, a border chief from the Strathclyde region, into the very parts of Ireland where Patrick was trying to preach. As an additional measure to disable the Irish, Vortigern married off his daughter, Scotnoe, to the son of the Irish king.

However, there is no evidence of cooperation or even interaction between Germanus and Vortigern. If

Germanus or another bishop did battle it would have been at the behest of the council of British aristocrats or British clergy, if it happened at all. Nevertheless, the slave raids and marriage to the Irish king's son were deft moves that reduced the threat of Irish raids. First problem solved.

Morris suggests that Vortigern had to deal with the Irish who had taken up residence in Wales and he called upon another border chief. Cunedda was a Romanized Briton like Vortigern. His grandfather, Paternus, was appointed by emperor Valentinian I to be chief of the Votadini tribe when the Romans still controlled the land all the way up to the Antonine Wall. The Votadini tribal area was on the east coast of the Scottish lowlands, in Godiddin, between Hadrian's Wall and the Antonine Wall. Cunedda's people were hard pressed by the Picts and needed a safer home. Morris claims Vortigern invited him to move to north Wales and wipe out the Irish settlers there. Cunedda accepted the offer and, with his sons and retainers, expelled the Irish settlers with great slaughter, according to Nennius.

Veprauskas offers a different view. He suggests that Vortigern wanted to station his Saxon friends (presumably Hengist and Horsa) in north Wales but the council objected. They did not want Saxons crossing through Britain to get to Wales nor did they want Vortigern's private army at their backs as well as their fronts. Vortigern acquiesced and offered the stronghold of Dinas Emrys and defense of northern Wales to Ambrosius the Elder. Ambrosius the Elder and the council trusted Cunedda more than they trusted the Saxons and it was Ambrosius who invited Cunedda to north Wales. (Nennius' inclusion of the fable about the two dragons and the grant of Dinas Emrys to a fatherless boy named Ambros is obviously a conflation of fact and fiction.)

Phillips and Keatman suggest that Cunedda moved to north Wales at the invitation of Ambrosius the Younger about 460. They arrive at this date calculating from the <u>Annales Cambriae</u>. Ashley places Cunedda's move closer to the early years of Vortigern's reign. He claims that Cunedda had been raiding south of Hadrian's Wall which brought him into conflict with Coel Hen (the original "Old King Cole"), the Romano-British commander at York. They negotiated a truce and Cunedda married Coel's daughter Gwawl. The terms of the truce are not known but Cunedda moved south shortly afterwards. Coel died about 430 so the move to north Wales had to be early in Vortigern's reign. Whoever invited Cunedda south, the establishment of a loyal, non-Saxon force in Gwynedd solved the problem of the Irish settlers .

There were still local Roman garrisons along Hadrian's wall, in the forts on the Saxon shore, and at York. They were not the prime Roman legions, but local national guard units under various local lords. The Picts presented Vortigern a difficult problem. Their raids were wiping out the garrisons on the east coast down as far as Norfolk. They had not yet breached Hadrian's Wall, but what was left of the northern garrisons was huddled in forts and towns and unwilling to secure the countryside. Vortigern was reluctant to lead his own war bands up north, fearing a coup from the aristocrats left at home in the south. So he asked the council to hire Saxon mercenaries to fight the Picts. The council gave its assent and in 428, three boatloads of Saxons arrived in the Thames estuary. This was, as noted above, a year before bishop Germanus arrived for his first visit to Britain.

The Saxons smashed the Picts so hard that they did not bother Britain for many years afterwards. Thus the third problem was solved but it had major consequences.

The Saxons

In chapter 15 of book 1, Bede describes the settlement areas of the Angles, Saxons, and Jutes. He writes that the Jutes settled Kent and the Isle of Wight. The Saxons settled East, South, and West Sussex. The Angles took over the most territory including East Anglia, Northrumbia, and Mercia. However the sources often call all of them Saxons or Angles without distinction and Bede even calls them English on one occasion. Gildas and Nennius call them all Saxons.

The chieftains of the three boatloads of Saxons who arrived in 428 were two brothers, Hengist and Horsa.   According to Nennius in chapter 36, "After the Saxons had continued sometime in the island of Thanet, Vortigern promised to supply them clothing and provision, on the condition that they would engage to fight against the enemies of his country" which in this case were the Picts who were sailing down the east coast from Scotland. We don't know precisely how long the Saxons had been on Thanet before Vortigern made this offer and we don't know if it was part of the deal when he, with the council's approval, invited them, or if the offer was "sometime" later. In the next sentence Nennius writes that the British council objected to the payment because the Saxon numbers had increased. Yet in the very next chapter 37, Hengist says "we are few in number; but if you will give us leave, we will send to our country for an additional number of forces, with whom we will fight for you and your subjects".

Nennius appears to have scrambled events. In 428-430 Vortigern was busy dealing with Irish raids and Cunedda was moving from Votadini territory north of Hadrian's Wall into Gwynedd. Bishop Germanus was in the country and Vortigern and the council had their hands full. It is likely that Vortigern and the council invited the Saxons with the intention of enlisting their help soon after Vortigern became overlord in 425. Vortigern welcomed them when they finally arrived in 428. Negotiations probably then began in how to use them and how to pay them. A deal was struck and the offer was made probably around 430. It was then that Hengist said "we are few in number . . ." and sent for many more warriors, It was only after the warriors arrived and sailed north to defeat the Picts, that Hengist demanded increased payment. Now there were many more than three boatloads of warriors whom the council originally agreed to pay, and they refused.

In chapter 37 Nennius describes the details. When Vortigern proposed the deal "Hengist, in whom united craft and penetration, perceiving he had to act with an ignorant king and a fluctuating people" brought over 16 boatloads of warriors and his daughter. He invited Vortigern to a banquet and had his daughter, Renwein, serve the head table. Vortigern was smitten by her and asked for her in marriage. (There is no record of what happened to Vortigern's first wife, Severa.) In return for his daughter, Vortigern granted Hengist the district of Kent. Nennius notes that he failed to notify Guoyranegonus, who governed Kent at the time!

Nennius reports that Hengist "after this" (at the banquet or a short time later) said to Vortigern "if you approve, I will send for my son and his brother, both valiant men, who at my invitation will fight against the Scots, and you can give

them the countries in the north, near the wall called *Gual*."
Vortigern did not control this area which he was giving
away, but that seemed not to bother him and besides, it had
just been vacated by Cunedda. He agreed. Octha and
Ebusa arrived with forty ships and sailed north to Scotland
where they crushed the Picts so thoroughly that they stayed
in their highlands for several generations afterwards. Octha
took over the former Votadini territory next to Hadrian's
wall. North of him a warlord named Germanianus took
control. This latter was a son of Coel Hen, the commander
at York.

Thus Vortigern, by clever manipulation or luck, solidified
his rule over southern Britain, wiped out his enemies to the
north and west, and established a system of alliances to
protect his kingdom.

But every solution often brings its own set of problems.
The gift of Kent to Hengist must certainly have shocked the
British council. It must have especially angered Ambrosius
the Elder who had nominal jurisdiction over the area. Also
Vortigern now possessed a powerful mercenary Saxon
army which could turn on them. The Saxon host had
swelled much larger than the original three boatloads and
by 437 they controlled Kent and the area north of Hadrian's
wall. No wonder the council refused.

This produced an open break between the council led by
Ambrosius the Elder and Vortigern. Bede placed the blame
for the break in religious terms, claiming that it was the
marriage between Vortigern and that Pagan woman,
Renwein. More likely it was the alienation of Kent without
council approval that produced the break. Bede writes:
"By this action he immediately incurred the enmity of his
leaders and, indeed, of his own sons . . . Angered with him
as they were, they promoted his son Vortimer to the

kingship." Bede gives no indication of a date for this promotion.

Nennius does not mention the promotion either but he does mention a quarrel at the end of his book, stuck in as if by afterthought: "And from the reign of Vortigern to the quarrel between Guitolinus and Ambrosius, are twelve years, which is Guoloppum, that is Catgwaloph." None of the other medieval writers or chronicles mention this quarrel. Morris, Alcock, and Veprauskas all characterize the quarrel as a battle near the town of Wallop, which is located in Hampshire, midway between London and Bath. They count the twelve years from the beginning of Vortigern's reign, placing the battle in 437. The only Ambrosius who would be active at that date was Ambrosius the Elder. The identity of Guitolinus is not known, but he is suspected to be a relative of Vortigern.

It is logical that the break between the council and Vortigern would result in civil strife and maybe even open civil war but there is another reading of Nennius. In the sentence before, he counts "from Stilicho to Valentinian, son of Placidia, and the reign of Vortigern, are twenty-eight years." If Nennius is counting from the end of Stilicho's reign in 408 he would arrive at 436 when Valentinian came of age. Therefore when he next writes "from the reign of Vortigern to the quarrel . . .", he could very well be counting from the end of Vortigern's reign, not the beginning. This would place the quarrel in 459 and the twelve years are those of Britu's rule from 447 after Vortigern's death to 459. This is the conclusion reached by Phillips and Keatman. Constable also puts the quarrel of Wallop in 459 and asserts that it was Ambrosius the Younger who fought Guitolinus.

The Saxon Revolt

The Saxons were not happy with the refusal by the council to give them supplies and they went on a rampage. Gildas writes "they (the Saxons) complain that their monthly supplies are not furnished in sufficient abundance, and . . .unless more liberality is shown them, they will break the treaty and plunder the whole island. In a short time, they follow up their threats with deeds." In 440 they raided Britain as recorded in the Gallic Chronicles quoted above. Gildas writes: "the fire of vengeance, . . . spread from sea to sea, fed by the hands of our foes in the east, and did not cease, until, destroying the neighboring towns and lands, it reached the other side of the island, and dipped its red and savage tongue in the western ocean."

The raid was not a conquest. Bede, copying Gildas, reports "When the victorious Angles scattered and destroyed the native peoples and returned to their own dwellings (in Kent and East Anglia), the Britons slowly began to take heart and recover their strength." Whether or not the quarrel at Wallop happened in 437 or 459, Ambrosius the Elder and the council most likely took effective charge of the Britons from 437 to 440. They may have formally deposed Vortigern soon after they learned of the alienation of Kent to the Saxons but they may not have been in any hurry to promote Britu to overlordship. For their part, the sons of Vortigern rebelled against their father and probably joined the council.

Ambrosius the Elder and most of his family were killed in the raid of 440. His son, Ambrosius the Younger, and many other Britons fled across the channel to Brittany. Bereft of leadership, the council may have turned at this juncture to Vortigern's eldest son. Britu assumed command and led the Britons in a counterattack. Nennius writes that Vortimer (Britu) rallied the Britons and forced the Saxons back to the Isle of Thanet three times. This would have been in 441 and whether the Saxons were forced back or merely followed back, they were holed up on Thanet.

Geoffrey claims that Vortigern fought on the side of the Saxons against his own sons and that he negotiated the departure of the Saxons who left for Germany. Geoffrey is exaggerating. The Saxons agreed to a truce but did not leave Thanet or East Anglia. William reports that the truce with the Saxons lasted seven years. It is likely that the truce was simply a lull in major fighting from 441 to 447 while Hengist gathered reinforcements. Britu probably used the time to build up his position. According to the monks, he embraced Christianity, repaired church property damaged in the raid, and may have received the blessing of Germanus who was in Britain in 447.

The Second Banquet

Hengist apparently used banquets as part of his strategy. At the first one, in the early 430's, he gave his daughter Renwein to Vortigern in exchange for Kent. At this second banquet, Hengist was constrained by Britu on Thanet after thrice retreating from the latter's counter attacks. By 446 he had likely received reinforcements and he now devised a different strategy to regain an edge. Nennius writes "with insidious intention they sent messengers to the king (Vortigern), with offers of peace and perpetual friendship; unsuspicious of treachery, the monarch, after advising with his elders, accepted the proposals." Nennius doesn't say, but one can imagine that Vortigern, deposed and friendless, might agree to any proposals that would restore him to power.

Hengist pointedly went over the head of Britu who commanded the British army but who may not have yet been promoted to overlordship. To seal the deal, Hengist invited Vortigern and his nobles to a banquet. Secretly he advised his own nobles each to hide a dagger on their person. When all had eaten and drunk, Hengist shouted out the signal, and the Saxons killed the Britons except Vortigern. Vortigern was spared because of his relationship with Hengist and also because he bought his release by giving the Saxons "East, South, and Middle Sex".

Neither Gildas nor Bede mention Hengist's second banquet. Geoffrey elaborates on Nennius' account and

William briefly mentions it. None of the sources specify a date. Nennius implies that it occurred after Britu died. Geoffrey adds that Renwein poisoned Britu and then alerted her father that he was dead, which gave Hengist the idea for the treacherous banquet. Nennius appears to have scrambled events again. It is much more likely that the banquet happened around 446 and Britu was still very much alive.

Renewed Hostilities

William contends that Britu broke the truce, perhaps on account of the murders at the banquet. This would have happened in 447. Nennius continues: "Four times did Vortimer (Britu) valorously encounter the enemy; the first has been mentioned, the second was on the river Darent, the third at the Ford, in their language called Epsford . . . there Horsa fell, and Categirn, the son of Vortigern; the fourth battle he fought, was near the stone on the shore of the Gallic sea, where the Saxons being defeated, fled to their ships". Geoffrey reports four pitched battles but lists only the last three of Nennius. Gildas and Bede are silent on the counterattack until the Ambrosius the Younger takes the field in 460.

The <u>Anglo-Saxon Chronicle</u> records four battles but in different order: the first in 455 in which "Hengist and Horsa fought Vortigern the king in the place called Aegelesthrep (Aylesford) his brother Horsa was killed", the second in 456 at Crecganford, the third in 465 at Wippedesfleot, and the fourth in 473 but not named. Constable notes that the difference between Nennius' list and the Chronicle may reflect the same series of battles remembered differently by the Welsh and Saxon writers. Bede, Nennius, and the <u>Anglo-Saxon Chronicle</u> all agree on at least one battle –Epiford/Aylesford – and the chronicle dates it at 455. They all agree that Horsa was killed there.

It is tempting to read Nennius and see his four battles as the quarrel at Wallop plus the three times he forced the Saxons back to Thanet. This may be where Geoffrey got the idea that the Saxons scrambled back to their ships and left for Germany. In fact Constable does identify the battles with locations in Kent. On the other hand, Bede places the arrival of the Saxons in 449 which may be the wave of reinforcements that Hengist had called, this time not for a raid, but to conquer. It is clear that many more Angles, Saxons, and Jutes arrived as the <u>Anglo-Saxon Chronicle</u> lists many more names: Aelle, Cerdic, and Cynric landing at different points and defeating Britons right and left. Therefore the efforts by Britu must be accounted between 447 and 455. Vermaat proposes that Britu died, probably in battle, shortly after 455.

The End of Vortigern

What happened to Vortigern after the banquet? Nennius reports two deaths for Vortigern. In chapter 47 he reports that Germanus returned from winning the Alleluia battle to chase Vortigern to the land of the Dimetae in southwest Wales where he had taken refuge in a stronghold called Cair Guothergirn on the river Towy in Wales.

Cair Guothergirn

There Germanus drew down fire from heaven - repeating the Benlii scenario – killing Vortigern and all his wives, a version Nennius took from Constantius's work. This claim led Phillips and Keatman to put Vortigern's death in the year 447, the last year Germanus was in Britain. Yet in chapter 48 Nennius claims that Vortigern "deserted and a wanderer, he sought a place of refuge, till broken hearted, he made an ignominious end."

Geoffrey tells a different story. He reports that after the
banquet massacre, all Britain rose against Vortigern, and he
fled to one of his strongholds in Wales. He writes that
Ambrosius the Younger returned from Brittany, raised an
army, and besieged Vortigern. Having failed to break
through the walls, he set fire to the fort and "burned up the
tower and Vortigern in it." So evidently Vortigern ended
his life burned to death in his stronghold – not by a
bishop's miracle but by a soldier's torch.

These two accounts – Nennius and Geoffrey – are the only
original sources that tell of Vortigern's death and they do
not offer a clear precise date. We know that Germanus was
in Britain in 447 and that he may have blessed Britu as
recorded on the Pillar of Eliseg but the story of his part in
Vortigern's death is a fable. Vermaat argues that Vortigern
died shortly after the banquet. If he died in 447, the twelve
years from then to 459 could be the reign of Vortigern the
Second (Britu). This means that it was Britu who fought
Hengist at Aylesford. The remaining battles listed in the
Anglo-Saxon Chronicle must have been fought by
Ambrosius the Younger. If Wallop happened in 459 after
Britu's death then Guitolinus may have been a relative
trying to step into his shoes but was thwarted by Ambrosius
the Younger.

Ambrosius the Younger lived into the 480's and if
Geoffrey is right, he was active in the death of Vortigern in
447. Thus his birth must have been in the late 420s when
Vortigern was welcoming Hengist and Horsa and while
Germanus was in Britain. An active life spanning sixty
years is perfectly within normal age limits.

Vortigern, an evaluation

Vortigern was born around 380 and died in 447 – an eventful 67 or so years. He was evidently wealthy and son of a powerful family. He was also ambitious. He married the daughter of Maximus and started rebuilding Virconium while still only the leader of the Cornovii tribe. He does not come across as either highly intelligent or charismatic. Nor does he appear to have been a great warrior. How was it that he came to power?

As Rome declined during the 4th Century, its authority in Britain waned in direct proportion to its power to defend the island and enforce the laws. The final blow came in 418 when the last Roman field forces left. However they did not leave a complete power vacuum. Some Roman officials remained, like Ambrosius the Elder. Some institutions remained like the council. Some form of collective decision making remained.

Two late Roman practices also remained: the appointment of a war leader distinct from the civil government in time of need and the incorporation of foreign fighters into the defense forces in trade for land. With the departure of regular Roman army units, the need was obvious and both practices would have seemed normal to the civilians and civil government left behind. However, there also remained Celtic tribal affiliations and family ties which may have been held back by formal Roman authority and enforcement, but which could come to the fore in their absence.

It is clear that government in Britain was in disarray, probably ever since Maximus left with his soldiers in 383. Gratianus Municeps briefly set himself up as dictator but was murdered in 407. The last Roman legion in Britain then proclaimed Constantine III as emperor and he marched off to Gaul where he was killed. The only authorities left in Britain were city magistrates, the large landowners, a few Roman officials, and the bishops. This evidently constituted the council – a collection of rivalries, individual agendas, petty egos, and general confusion. The economy had reverted to local supply and demand with little extra to pay for a field force.

Into this confusion, Vortigern probably put himself forward as the leader. He was wealthy and had the force of his Cornovii tribe to back him up. He wanted the job and perhaps offered warriors from his tribe. Whatever the case, he became the ruler in 425. At first, he and the council appeared to be able to work together. He was keenly aware of his base in Powys and was willing to compromise to protect it. He was able to work with Ambrosius the Elder and even let him arrange for the defense of north Wales. He also won council approval to recruit the Saxons to help defend against the Picts. He does not appear to have had any bigger goal than to achieve the position of leader. He does not appear to have had a vision or a plan for the future of the realm. Had there been peace and a decent economy – and no squabbling churchmen – he may have had an uneventful reign.

However the challenges of his time were bigger than his abilities. He feared for the instability of his position vis a vis the council more than he appreciated the larger danger of the Saxons. He gravitated to the latter who theoretically owed allegiance only to him as opposed to the council where he may always have felt and was treated as an outsider. Hengist was clever and played Vortigern with the result that he depended on the Saxons more than upon the council. In the end, Hengist betrayed him and Vortigern had no one left to support him, not even his sons. He fled to Cair Guothergirn where Ambrosius the Younger put an end to his rule and his life.

Bibliography

Primary Sources:

Gildas: De Exidio Brittaniae. translated by J. A. Giles

Constantius of Lyon: Life of St. Germanus in www.vortigernstudies.org. (2008)

Prosper of Aquitaine: Epitoma Chronicon in From Roman to Merovingian Gaul: A Reader translated and edited by A. C. Murray (2003)

Nennius: Historia Brittonum translated J. A. Giles

Geoffrey of Monmouth: The History of the Kings of Britain translated Lewis Thorpe (1966)

The Anglo-Saxon Chronicles translated and collated by Anne Savage (1988)

The Annales Cambriae translated by James Ingram. (1912) www.vortigernstudies.org. (2008)

The Mabinogion. translated by Jeffrey Gantz. (1976)

Secondary Sources:

Alcock, Leslie: Arthur's Britain – History and Archeology 367-634. (1989)

Ashe, Geoffrey: The Quest for Arthur's Britain. (1971)

Ashley, Mike: King Arthur. (2005)

Blake, Steve and Lloyd, Scott: The Keys to Avalon.
(2000)

Constable, Patrick: Discordia at www.vortigernstudies.org

Ford, David: Vortigern and His Family at
www.vortigernstudies.org

Morris, John: The Age of Arthur. (1973)

Phillips, Graham & Keatman, Martin: King Arthur – The
True Story (1992)

Scullard, H. H.: Roman Britain. (1979)

Veprauskas, Michael: The Problem of Caer Guorthigirn at
www.vortigernstudies.org

Veprauskas, Michael: The Generations of Ambrosius at
www.vortigernstudies.org

Veprauskas, Michael: Adventus Saxonum at
www.earlybritishkingdoms.com/articles

Vermaat, Robert, ed: Vortigern Studies at
www.vortigernstudies.org.